Down & Dirty
The Secrets of Soil

What's Soil Made Of?

by Ellen Lawrence

Consultant:

Shawn W. Wallace
Department of Earth and Planetary Sciences
American Museum of Natural History, New York, New York

BEARPORT PUBLISHING

New York, New York

Credits

Cover, © gkuna/Shutterstock, © Nipon-Photo/Shutterstock, © balounm/Shutterstock, and © Kokhanchikov/Shutterstock; 4T, © Liudmila Savushkina/Shutterstock; 4B, © Joe Gough/Shutterstock; 5, © Ivan Kruk/Shutterstock; 6, © Merkushev Vasiliy/Shutterstock; 7, © D. Kucharski K. Kucharska/Shutterstock; 8, © Thawornnurak/Shutterstock; 9, © Jose Ramiro Laguna/Shutterstock; 10, © Szabi/Shutterstock; 11, © Marc Venema/Shutterstock and © Thirteen/Shutterstock; 12, © Margaret M. Stewart/Shutterstock; 13TL, © Dave Allen Photography/Shutterstock; 13BL, © Anatolii Lyzun/Shutterstock; 13R, © Sarah Marchant/Shutterstock; 14, © Vishnevskiy Vasily/Shutterstock; 15, © Gerard Lacz/FLPA; 16T, © Piotr Naskrecki/Minden Pictures/FLPA; 16B, © Ljupco Smokovski/Shutterstock; 17, © Eye of Science/Science Photo Library; 18, © ifong/Shutterstock; 19, © Animals Animals/Superstock; 20T, © aodaodaodaod/Shutterstock; 20B, © Krit Leoniz/Shutterstock; 21, © Aleksei Sarkisov/Shutterstock; 22, © nanD_Phanuwat/Shutterstock and © Alexey Losevich/Shutterstock; 23TL, © Thirteen/Shutterstock; 23TR, © Eye of Science/Science Photo Library; 23BL, © wavebreakmedia/Shutterstock; 23BR, © balounm/Shutterstock.

Publisher: Kenn Goin
Editor: Jessica Rudolph
Creative Director: Spencer Brinker
Design: Emma Randall
Photo Researcher: Ruby Tuesday Books Ltd

Library of Congress Cataloging-in-Publication Data

Lawrence, Ellen, 1967– author.
  What's soil made of? / by Ellen Lawrence.
      pages cm. — (Down & dirty : the secrets of soil)
  Audience: Ages 7-12.
  Summary: "In this book, readers learn what makes up soil."— Provided by publisher.
  Includes bibliographical references and index.
  ISBN 978-1-62724-834-1 (library binding : alk. paper) — ISBN 1-62724-834-X (library binding : alk. paper)
  1. Soil science—Juvenile literature. 2. Soil formation—Juvenile literature. 3. Soils—Juvenile literature. I. Title. II. Title: What is soil made of.
  S591.3.L3875 2016
  631.4—dc23
                              2015017878

For more information, write to Bearport Publishing Company, Inc., 45 West 21st Street, Suite 3B, New York, New York 10010. Printed in the United States of America.

10 9 8 7 6 5 4 3 2 1

Contents

Soil All Around

What can be brown, yellow, red, crumbly, wet, or sticky? Soil!

Soil is where plants grow and where many animals make their homes.

In fact, people, plants, and animals all need soil to live.

So where does soil come from, and what is it made of? Let's find out!

soil in a yard

peanut plants growing in soil

It's not always possible to see soil in a city, but it's there. Houses, apartments, schools, roads, and sidewalks are all built on top of soil.

a construction site in a city

soil

A Close-Up Look at Soil

A handful of soil can feel soft and crumbly.

So it might be hard to believe that the main **ingredient** in soil is rock!

Sometimes, pieces of rock in soil are big enough to see.

Most of the pieces of rock, however, are tiny grains.

Where does the rock come from?

a rock

tiny grains of rock

an earthworm in soil

Many of the tiny pieces of rock in soil are the size of grains of salt. Some pieces of rock are so tiny they can only be seen through a **microscope**.

Earth's Surface

Earth's surface is made up of soil and rock.

In most places, there's a layer of soil where plants grow.

Below the soil is a layer of rock.

In some places, such as mountains, the rocky layer can be seen.

Over time, changes to the rocky layer help create soil.

grass growing in soil on top of a rocky cliff

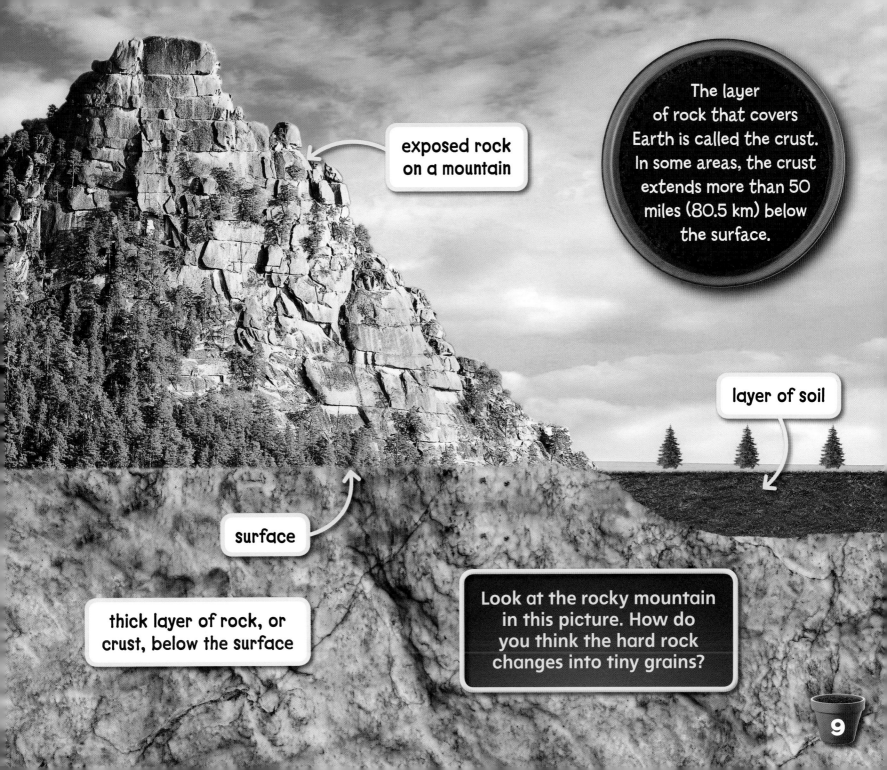

exposed rock
on a mountain

The layer of rock that covers Earth is called the crust. In some areas, the crust extends more than 50 miles (80.5 km) below the surface.

layer of soil

surface

thick layer of rock, or crust, below the surface

Look at the rocky mountain in this picture. How do you think the hard rock changes into tiny grains?

Rain and Wind

Rain can cause mountains and other rocks to change. How?

As water flows or trickles down a mountain, it wears away the rock.

Billions of tiny grains of rock break off and get washed down the mountain.

The pieces of rock collect at the bottom of the mountain and then become soil.

rainwater flowing down a mountain

Rocks can also be changed by the wind. Pieces of dust in the wind rub against mountains and large rocks, causing tiny grains of rock to break off. These grains fall to the ground and then become soil.

bits of rock at the bottom of a mountain

Dead Plants

Dead plants are also an important part of soil.

An ingredient in soil that was once living or came from a living thing is called **organic** material.

When plants die or leaves fall from trees, they lie on the ground.

Over several months, the plants and leaves rot and become crumbly.

Then they mix with bits of rock and become part of the soil.

As animals such as chipmunks dig underground homes, they churn up the bits of rock and dead plants on the surface of the ground. This helps the ingredients mix and become soil.

Leaves and twigs fall to the ground.

It's not just plants that become part of the soil— animals do, too. How do you think this happens?

The leaves and twigs start to rot.

The bits of plants become part of the soil.

13

Bones, Feathers, and Poop

There's another kind of organic material that makes up soil—the bodies of dead animals.

When an animal dies, its body breaks down on the ground.

It might take a long time, but eventually the body rots.

Then, tiny pieces of feathers, fur, bones, and other body parts mix in with the soil.

a dead bird on the ground

Another organic ingredient in soil is poop! When animals leave poop on the ground, it rots and becomes part of the soil.

rhino poop

What's Living in Soil?

The ingredients that make up soil may not be alive.

However, soil has lots of life in it.

Ants, millipedes, worms, and many other animals live in soil.

Soil is also home to **microbes**—living things that are too small to see without a microscope.

Microbes help to break down organic material.

millipede

ants

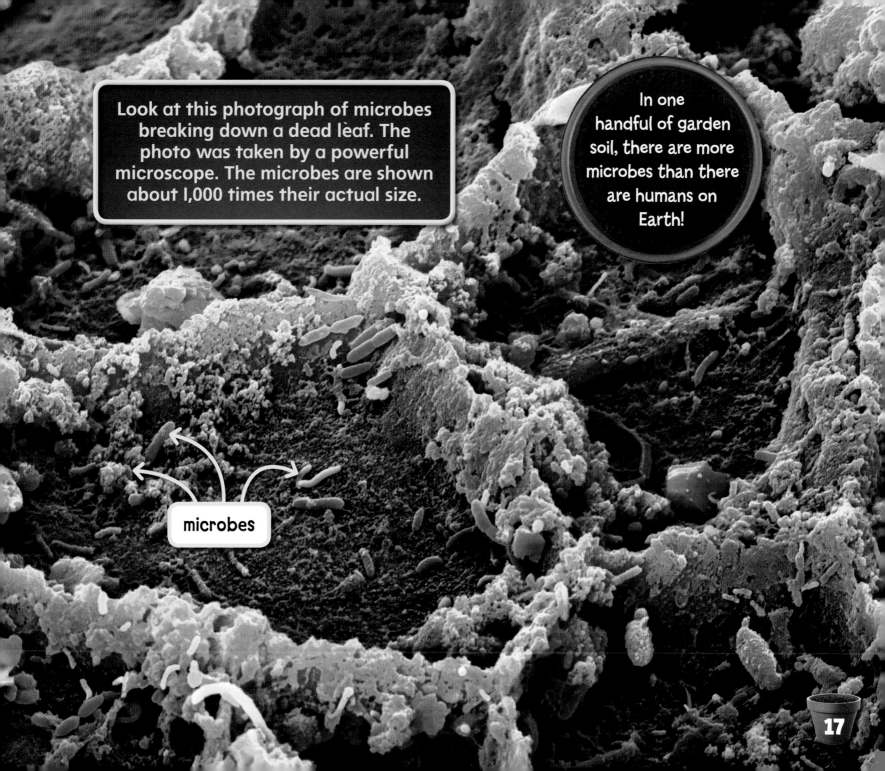

Look at this photograph of microbes breaking down a dead leaf. The photo was taken by a powerful microscope. The microbes are shown about 1,000 times their actual size.

In one handful of garden soil, there are more microbes than there are humans on Earth!

microbes

Air and Water

There are two other important substances in soil—air and water.

Soil contains many tiny spaces.

When rain falls or snow melts, water trickles down into these gaps.

Air gets into the soil, too, and collects in the tiny spaces.

Plants and animals in soil need this air and water to survive.

roots

Plants take in water from the soil through their roots.

As worms wriggle around underground, they move the soil. They help create tiny tunnels where air and water can collect.

a worm making a tunnel in the soil

tiny spaces

In this book you've seen soil that's orange, brown, and rocky. Why do you think soil can have different looks?

19

Different Types of Soil

All soil is made of rock and organic material, but it doesn't all look alike.

The soil in a desert may be orange because it contains bits of orange rock.

The soil in a forest might be dark and squishy.

That's because it contains wet, rotted leaves and very little rock.

It's the different mixtures of ingredients that give soil its many appearances!

forest soil

It can take up to 500 years for just 1 inch (2.5 cm) of soil to form.

orange soil in a desert

What's in Soil?

Find out what ingredients are in a cup of soil.

I. Empty a cup of soil onto a sheet of white paper. Spread out the soil and look closely at it with a magnifying glass.

2. Using tweezers and your fingers, separate the things you find into three categories:
   - Nonliving: for example, stones or bits of rock
   - Once living: organic material, such as leaves or dead insects
   - Living: animals, such as worms or beetles

   If you find a living thing, carefully pick it up and put it into a jar.

3. In your notebook, list all the things you find.

4. When you have finished your investigation, put the animals and soil back outside, then wash your hands.

> **You will need:**
> - A cup of soil
> - A sheet of white paper
> - A magnifying glass
> - Tweezers
> - A jar with a lid
> - A notebook and pencil

Science Words

ingredient (in-GREE-dee-int) one of the substances that something is made from; bits of rock are an ingredient in soil

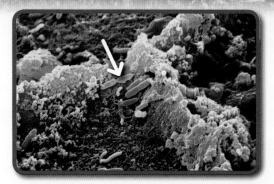

microbes (MYE-krohbz) extremely tiny living things that can only be seen with a microscope; some microbes break down organic material

microscope (MYE-kruh-skohp) a tool used to see things that are too small to see with the eyes alone

organic (or-GAN-ik) a material that was once living, such as dead leaves or the body of an animal

Index

Read More

Lawrence, Ellen. *Dirt (FUN-damental Experiments)*. New York: Bearport (2013).

Owen, Ruth. *Science and Craft Projects with Rocks and Soil (Get Crafty Outdoors)*. New York: Rosen (2013).

Schuh, Mari. *Soil Basics (Pebble Plus)*. North Mankato, MN: Capstone Press (2012).

Learn More Online

To learn more about what soil is made of, visit
www.bearportpublishing.com/Down&Dirty

About the Author

Ellen Lawrence lives in the United Kingdom. Her favorite books to write are those about animals and nature. In fact, the first book Ellen bought for herself, when she was six years old, was the story of a gorilla named Patty Cake that was born in New York's Central Park Zoo.